Infantry Training

RIFLE AND BAYONET
1954

This pamphlet is produced for West Africa Command

Crown Copyright Reserved

By Command of the Army Council

THE WAR OFFICE

3rd MARCH, 1954

The Naval & Military Press Ltd

Published by

The Naval & Military Press Ltd

Unit 5 Riverside, Brambleside,
Bellbrook Industrial Estate,
Uckfield, East Sussex,
TN22 1QQ England

Tel: +44 (0) 1825 749494
Fax: +44 (0) 1825 765701

www.naval-military-press.com
www.nmarchive.com

The Library & Archives Department at the Royal Armouries Museum, Leeds, specialises in the history and development of armour and weapons from earliest times to the present day. Material relating to the development of artillery and modern fortifications is held at the Royal Armouries Museum, Fort Nelson.

For further information contact:
Royal Armouries Museum, Library, Armouries Drive, Leeds, West Yorkshire LS10 1LT
Royal Armouries, Library, Fort Nelson, Down End Road, Fareham PO17 6AN

Or visit the Museum's website at
www.armouries.org.uk

In reprinting in facsimile from the original, any imperfections are inevitably reproduced and the quality may fall short of modern type and cartographic standards.

Infantry Training

RIFLE AND BAYONET

1954

CONTENTS

		Page
Lesson 1.	The Rifle. Stripping, assembling and sightsetting	1
Lesson 2.	The Rifle. Care and cleaning	6
Lesson 3.	Loading and unloading	10
Lesson 4.	Lying position and hold	16
Lesson 5.	Aiming. Range targets	19
Lesson 6.	Trigger control	24
Lesson 7.	Firing a shot	26
Lesson 8.	On guard and hip firing	30
Lesson 9.	The point	32
Lesson 10.	Alteration of sights	37
Lesson 11.	Two points	39
Lesson 12.	Working the bolt	43
Lesson 13.	Further cleaning	46
Lesson 14.	Snapshooting	49
Lesson 15.	Rapid firing	52
Lesson 16.	The training stick	55
Lesson 17.	Firing from other positions	59
Lesson 18.	Self-defence	62

LESSON 1
THE RIFLE. STRIPPING, ASSEMBLING AND SIGHTSETTING

Lesson

Identification, stripping, assembling, and sightsetting

Stores

Rifles   Bayonets   Drill cartridges

Teach

RIFLE MUST NOT BE LOADED

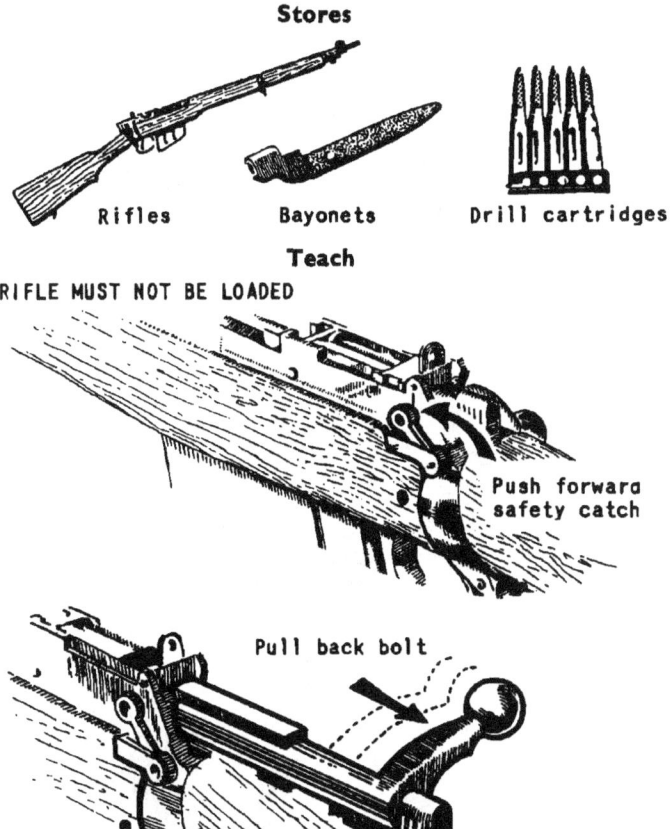

Push forward safety catch

Pull back bolt

See that magazine and chamber are clear

Close bolt

Squeeze trigger

Pull back safety catch

IDENTIFY

Nos. on bolt and rifle must be the same

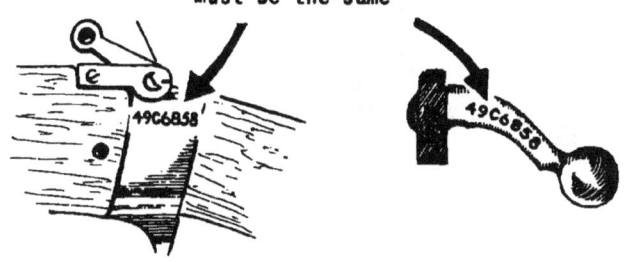

STRIPPING

Remove bayonet and scabbard

Remove the sling

Remove the bolt

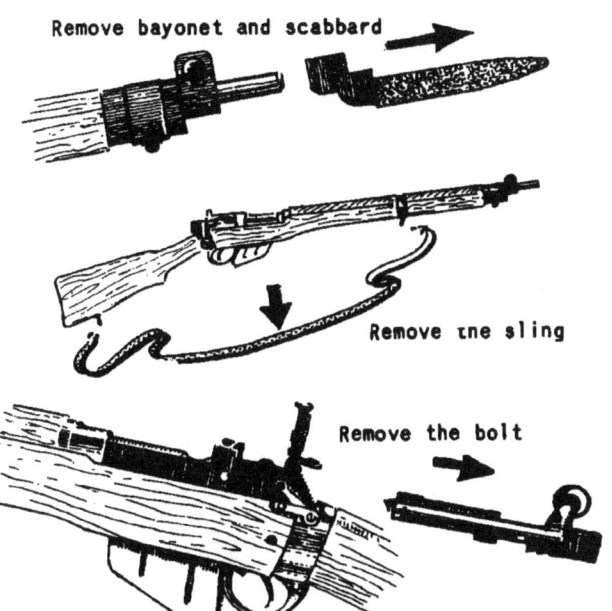

4

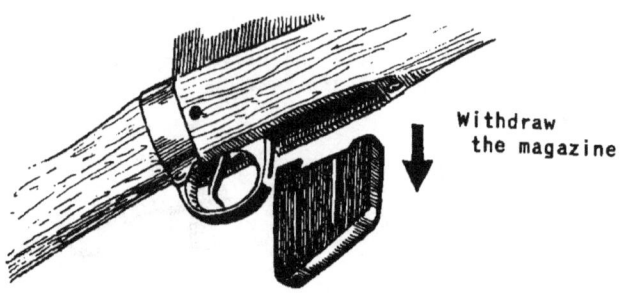

Withdraw the magazine

ASSEMBLING

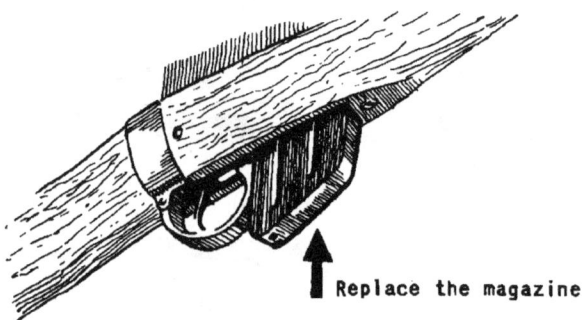

Replace the magazine

Replace the bolt

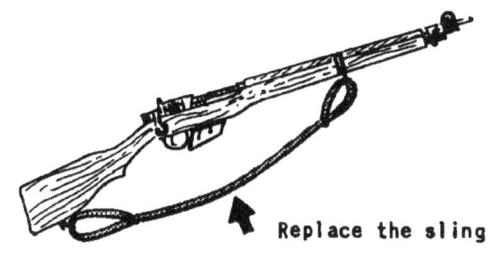

Replace the sling

Replace the bayonet and scabbard

SIGHTSETTING

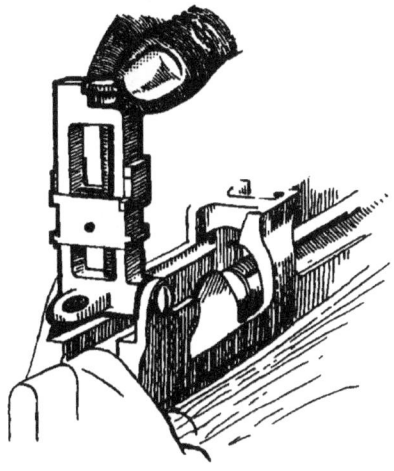

Practise squad

LESSON 2
THE RIFLE. CARE AND CLEANING

Lesson

Care and cleaning

Stores

Oil bottle

Flannelette

Rag

Rifle

Pull-through

Chamber cleaning stick

Practise lesson 1

Teach

RIFLE MUST BE CLEANED AND OILED TO KEEP IT SHOOTING WELL

Open butt trap and take out
(a) Pull-through
(b) Oilbottle

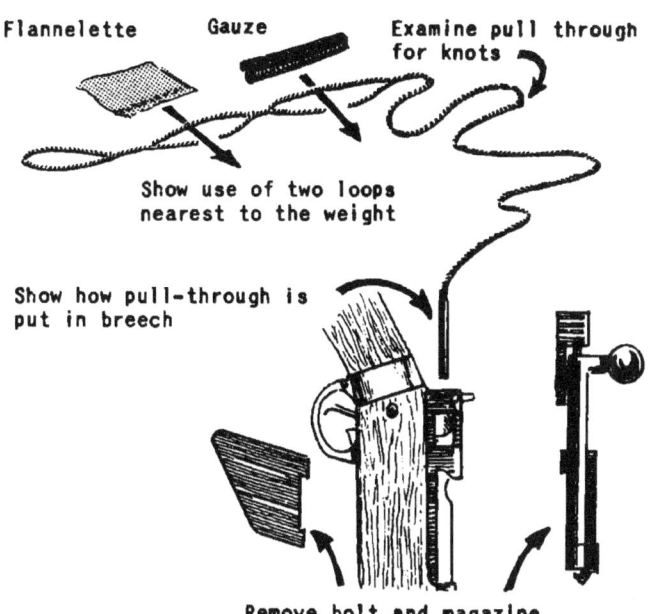

Flannelette   Gauze   Examine pull through for knots

Show use of two loops nearest to the weight

Show how pull-through is put in breech

Remove bolt and magazine

Pull rifle through like this

Show need for STRAIGHT pull through to prevent cord wear

DAILY CLEANING

Pull rifle through DRY

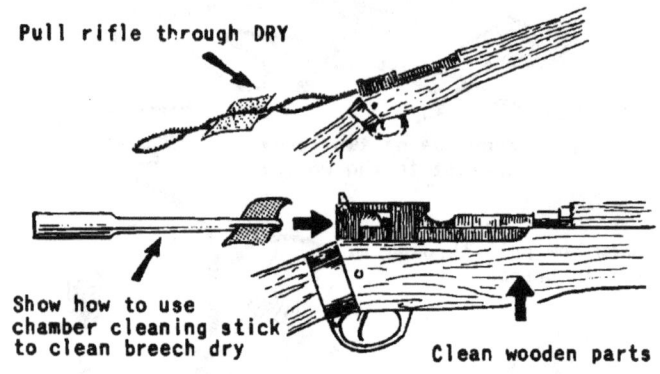

Show how to use chamber cleaning stick to clean breech dry

Clean wooden parts

Look through rifle from muzzle and from breech

Pull rifle through with oily flannelette 4 in. x 1½ in.

Clean and oil breech

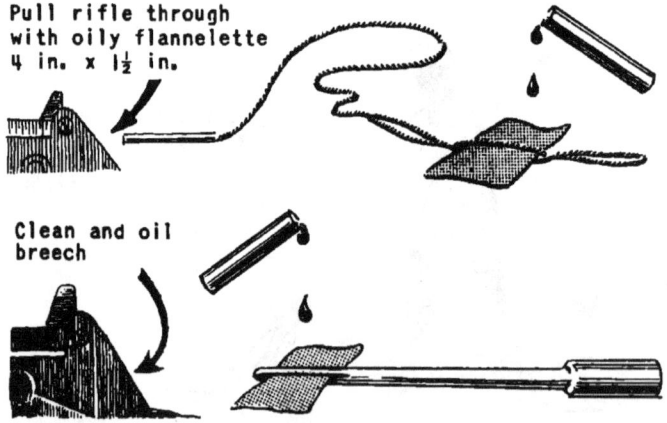

Clean and oil bolt

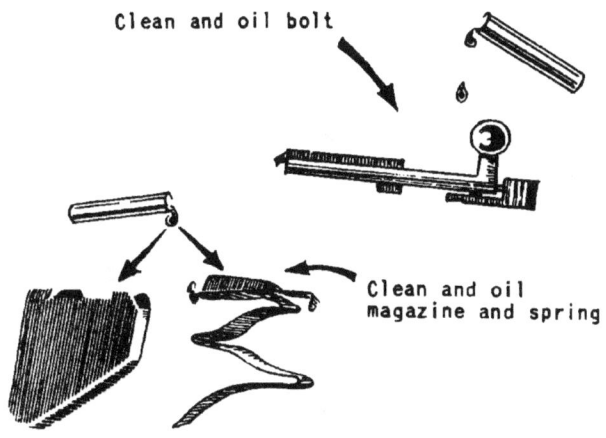

Clean and oil magazine and spring

ASSEMBLY

Put each part back as it is cleaned

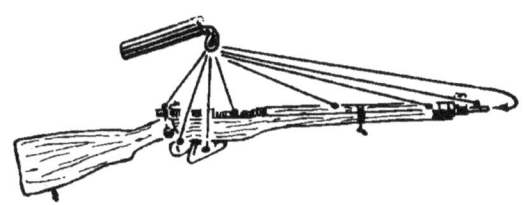

Roll up pull-through and put it in butt trap

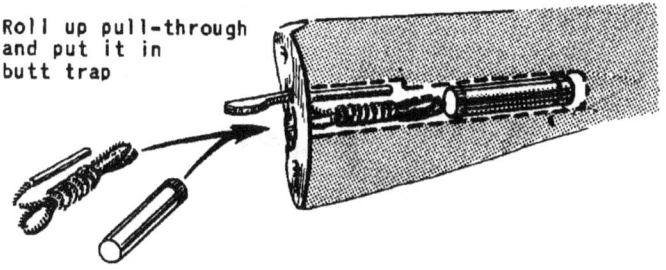

LESSON 3
LOADING AND UNLOADING

Lessons

Clean ammunition and the correct filling of chargers
Loading and unloading

Stores

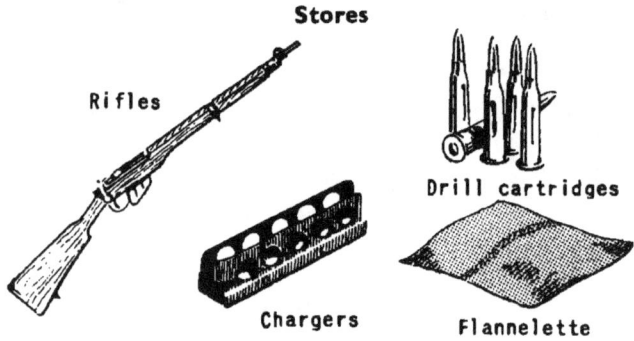

Rifles

Drill cartridges

Chargers

Flannelette

Teach

The rifle will not fire rapid if the ammunition is not clean
Show squad how to clean ammunition and fill chargers

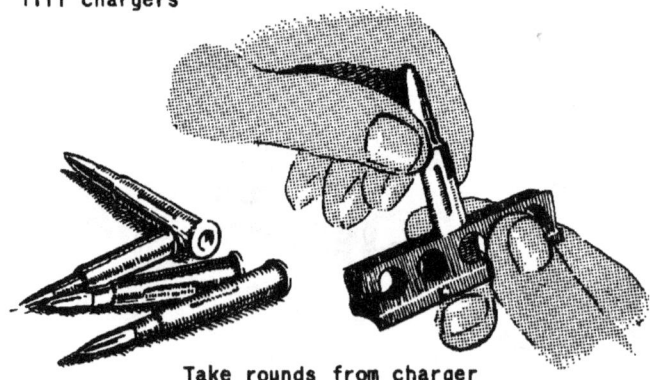

Take rounds from charger

11

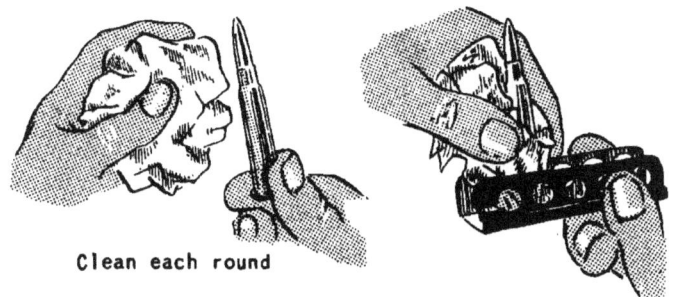

Clean each round

Clean the charger

Load charger one UP one DOWN

TO LOAD

Always point the muzzle upwards like this

Open bolt pull back

Put charger in guide and press down with thumb

Take out empty charger

Close bolt

Pull back safety catch

If a round does not go into chamber press down on the rounds sharply on top of the magazine

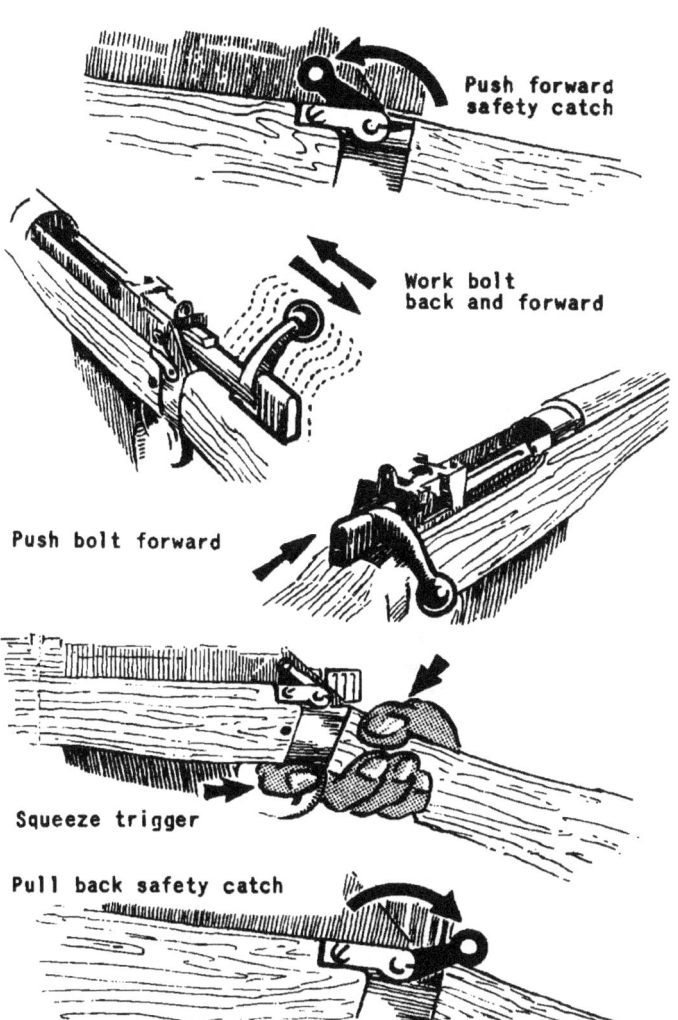

14

LYING LOAD

Like this

Load rifle as already taught

FILL MAGAZINE

This means:- All rounds in magazine
No round in breech

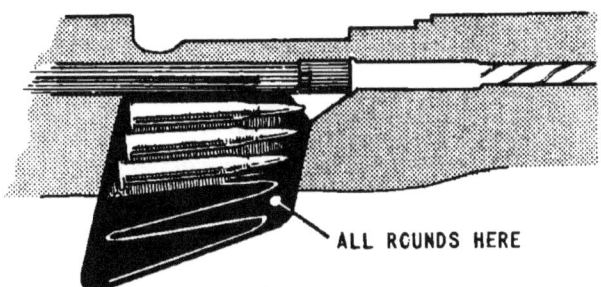

ALL ROUNDS HERE

Two ways to fill magazine

(a) Press down rounds with left thumb
and
Close bolt with right hand over the top of the rounds

(b)

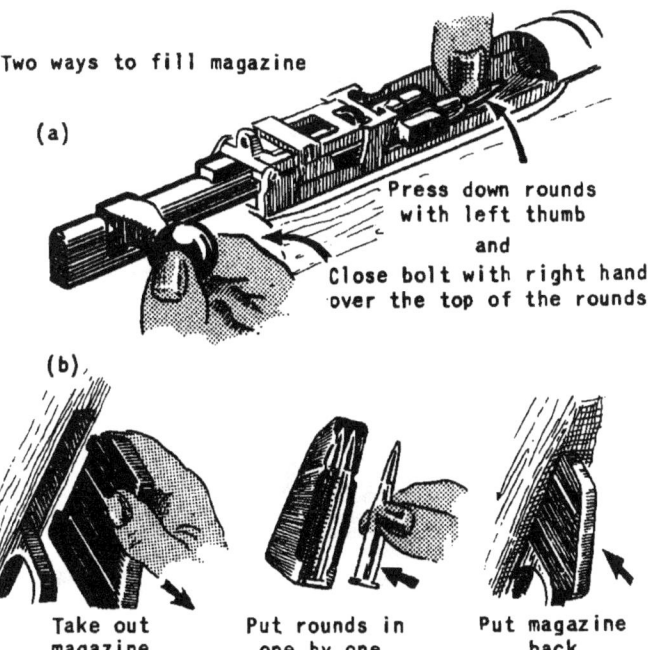

Take out magazine

Put rounds in one by one

Put magazine back

LESSON 4

LYING POSITION AND HOLD

Lesson

To teach how to hold the rifle in the firing position

Stores

Rifles

Teach

THE BEST POSITION TO FIRE FROM IS THE LYING POSITION
The rifle must be held firmly
Aim must be right
When the trigger is pulled the aim must not be moved

Show the lying position

Arms must be well apart

Butt in shoulder

Cheek in butt

Right hand on butt very tight and pull back to shoulder

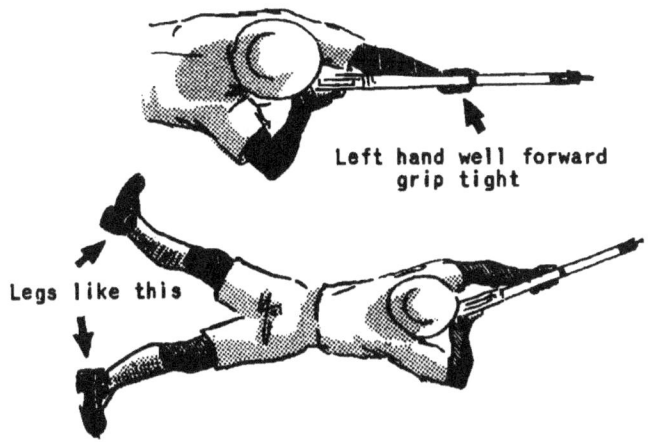
Left hand well forward grip tight

Legs like this

BREATHING

Tell squad. Do not breathe when taking aim
Show how breathing makes rifle go up and down

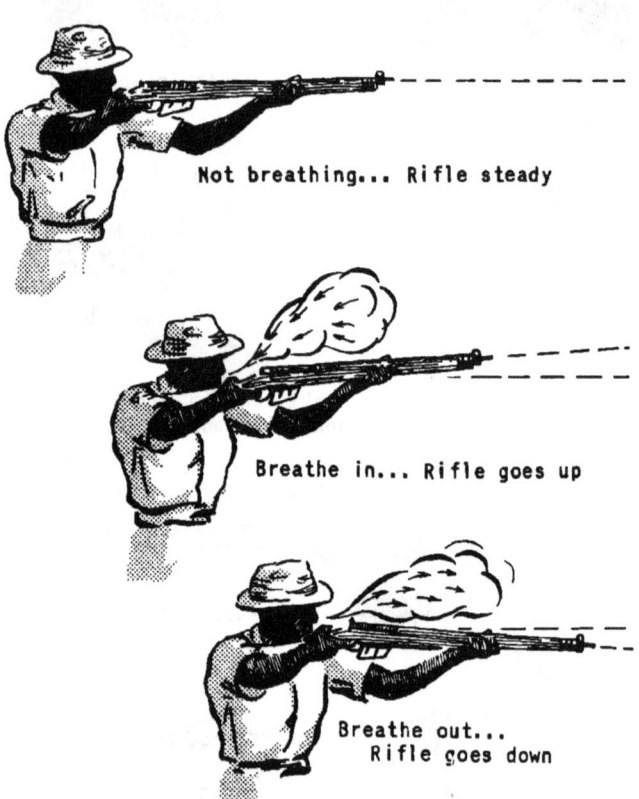

Not breathing... Rifle steady

Breathe in... Rifle goes up

Breathe out... Rifle goes down

Practise squad and check each man

Make sure each man has a comfortable position

LESSON 5
AIMING. RANGE TARGETS

Lesson

To teach the correct aim
To teach aiming at targets

Stores

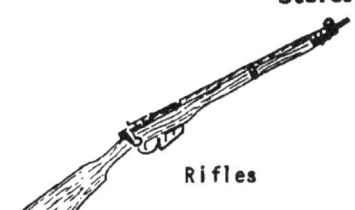

Rifles

Aiming rests

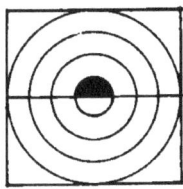

Range targets

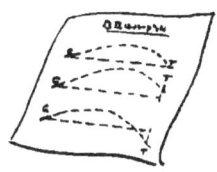

Diagrams

Teach

CHECK

Backsight is not loose

Backsight aperture and foresight blade is correct

TEACH RULES OF AIMING

(a) Close left eye

(b) Look through aperture at the target and see the point of aim

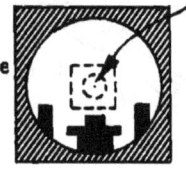

Point of aim

(c) Bring up foresight in line with the point of aim

(d) Keep point of aim in line with centre of aperture

NOT THIS

THIS

(e) Keep sights upright

AIMING REST

Set up with one leg towards the target

Squad to copy

THE CORRECT AIM

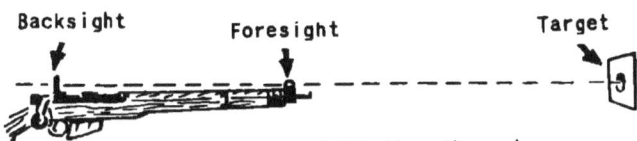

Must be a straight line through

LAYING THE AIM

Show correct aim with range target

ELBOW REST

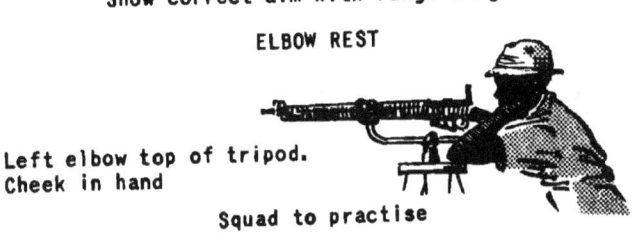

Left elbow top of tripod.
Cheek in hand

Squad to practise

FLIGHT OF THE BULLET

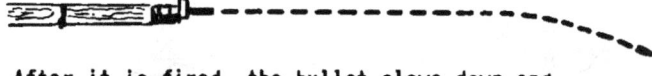

After it is fired, the bullet slows down and
begins to drop just as a stone will when thrown.

To make the bullet hit the target the
rifle must be cocked up - this will over-
come the drop of the bullet.

SIGHTS

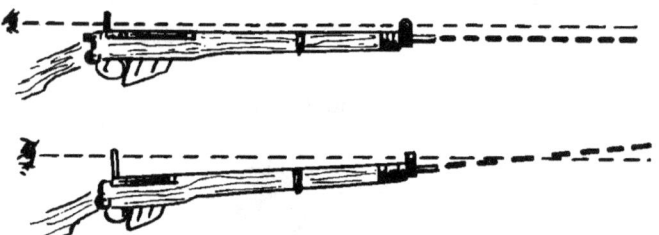

The rifle is cocked up and down by means
of the sights

DEMONSTRATION OF FLIGHT OF BULLET
Two rifles in rests

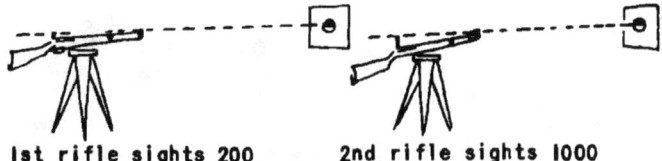

1st rifle sights 200   2nd rifle sights 1000

23

Take out bolts

Look through barrels

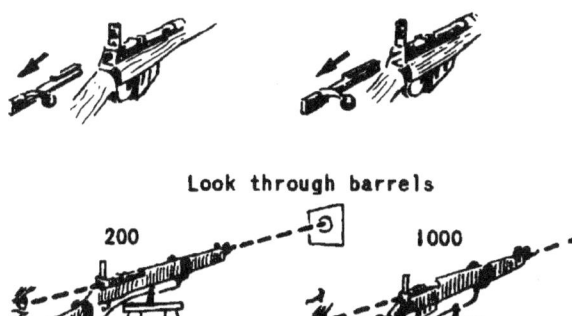

1st rifle barrel will point at target

2nd rifle barrel will point above target

TEACH SQUAD

Both sights are on aiming marks

The rifle which is cocked up over the target has sights at 1000.

If the target were also at 1000 the bullet would then hit it.
Practise squad.

LESSON 6
TRIGGER CONTROL

Lesson

How to operate the trigger without disturbing the aim

Stores

Rifles

Pennies

Teach

When the trigger is operated the aim may be changed.
This will not happen if the right hand is made strong.
These exercises will make it strong.

EXERCISE 1

Grip left wrist tightly with the right hand

Press wrist gently with the trigger finger

When the finger is pressed down and the rest of the hand does not tighten the grip is correct

EXERCISE 2

Close the right hand and rest on knee.

Hold trigger finger like this.

Move it as for trigger pressing.

The only movement should be from here.

EXERCISE 3

Lying position with rifle in shoulder and action cocked

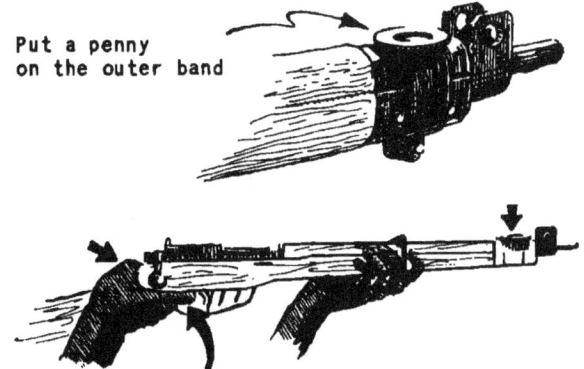

Put a penny on the outer band

The trigger is squeezed without knocking the penny off

LESSON 7
FIRING A SHOT

Lessons

To teach the drill for firing a shot
Prepare for miniature range

Stores

Rifles

Drill cartridges

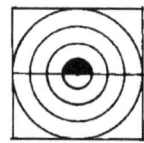
Targets

Stick rests

Teach

Ask squad for three rules of shooting

STICK REST

Show correct use of it.   Like this

The stick rest is to steady the rifle.   Do not press against it, it will cause bad aiming.
Practise squad

POINT BODY AT THE TARGET

When holding the rifle in a comfortable firing position the hands should point at the target

If they do not, move the body until they do

Practise squad

PREPARE TO FIRE

Test that firer's body is pointing at target

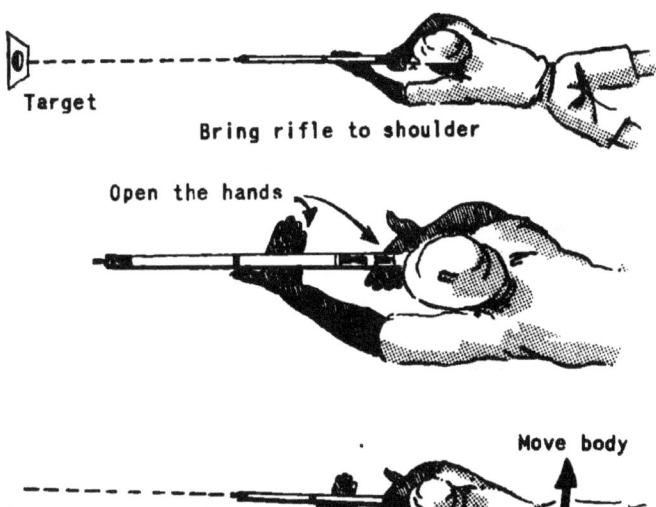

Bring rifle to shoulder

Open the hands

Move body

Target

If the rifle moves off the target the body is not pointing correctly

TO RAISE OR LOWER THE RIFLE

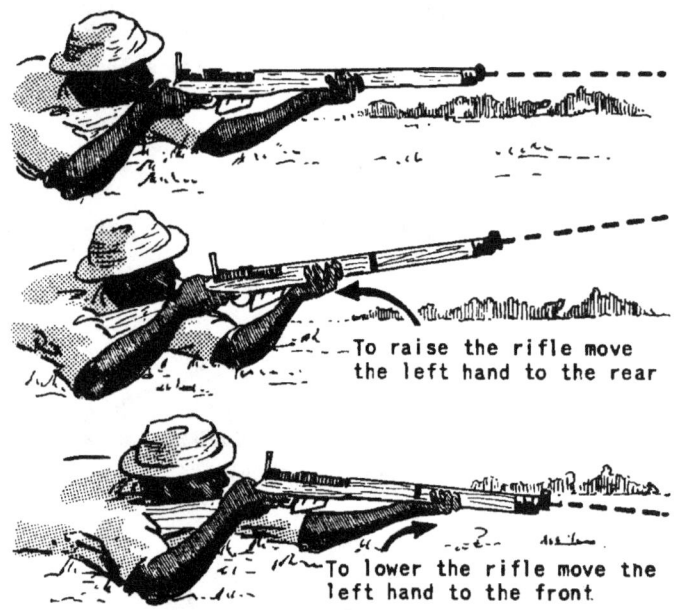

To raise the rifle move the left hand to the rear

To lower the rifle move the left hand to the front

FIRING A SHOT

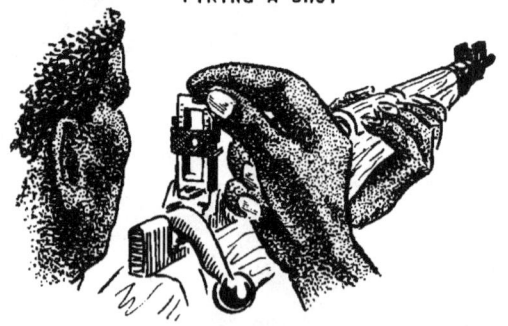

Put range on sights

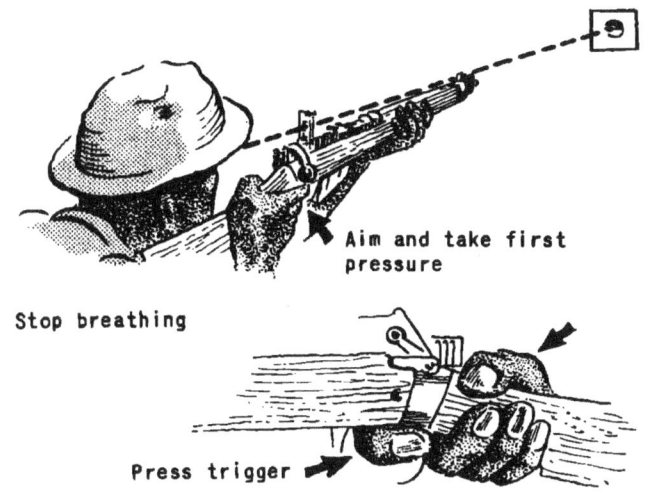

Aim and take first pressure

Stop breathing

Press trigger

Do not remain in aim for more than a slow count of three

Reload in shoulder

Come down from aim

Practise squad

LESSON 8
ON GUARD AND HIP FIRING

Lessons

The on guard position
Firing from the hip

Stores

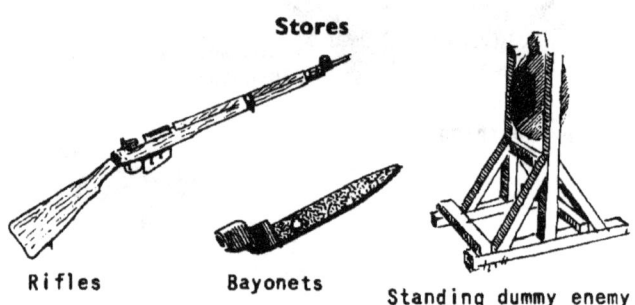

Rifles   Bayonets   Standing dummy enemy

Teach

SHOW THE ON GUARD POSITION

Left hand firmly on the outer band

Butt tight against side of body

Right hand firmly on small of butt

REST

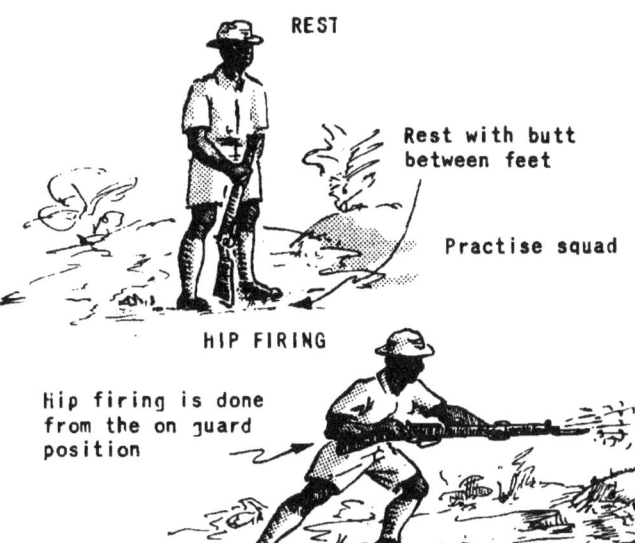

Rest with butt between feet

Practise squad

HIP FIRING

Hip firing is done from the on guard position

RELOADING

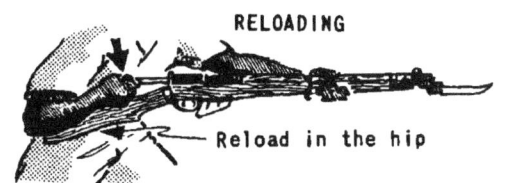

Reload in the hip

CARRIAGES OF RIFLE

Across front of body

At the trail

Practise squad

LESSON 9
THE POINT

Lesson

To teach the point at an enemy standing or lying on the ground

Stores

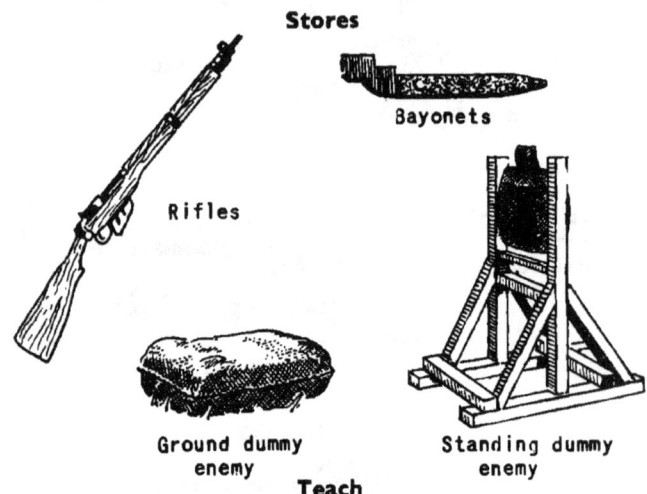

Bayonets

Rifles

Ground dummy enemy

Standing dummy enemy

Teach

SHOW SQUAD THE POINT

Form squad in front of dummies

GIVE ORDERS

On guard

Point

Withdraw

On guard

Pass through

Practise squad

At walk   At double

GROUND ENEMY

Point at dummy

Keep feet off dummy

Put left foot on dummy

Pull bayonet out

On guard

Pass through

Practise squad

LESSON 10
ALTERATION OF SIGHTS

Lesson
To correct errors in elevation

Stores

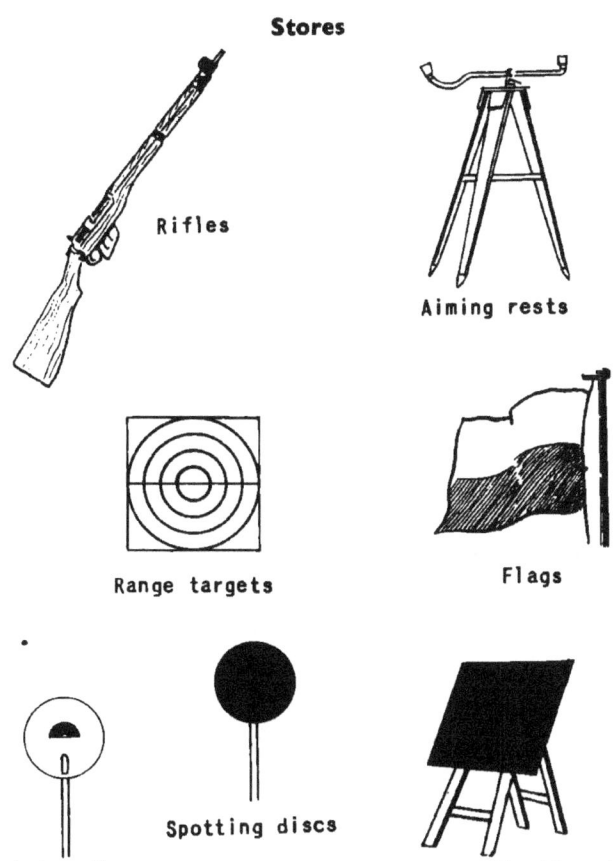

Rifles

Aiming rests

Range targets

Flags

Aiming discs

Spotting discs

Charts or blackboards

Teach

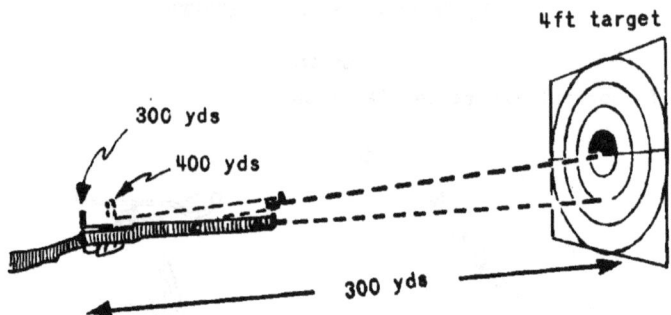

At 300 yds each 100 yds change on backsight means this:-

Practise squad by giving position of shot on target and asking for sight correction

LESSON 11
TWO POINTS

Lesson

How to deal with two enemy quickly

Stores

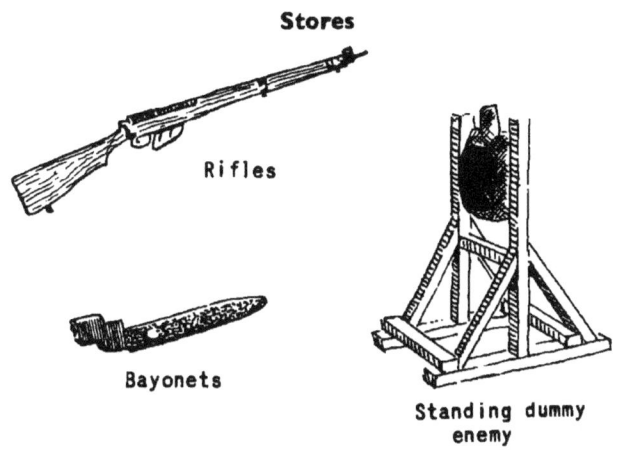

Rifles

Bayonets

Standing dummy enemy

Teach

Put out dummies and squad

ORDERS

Front rank on guard

Point at 1

Withdraw

Point at 2

Withdraw

On guard

Pass through

Practise squad

Teach ground dummies mixed with standing dummies

LESSON 12
WORKING THE BOLT

Lesson

To teach the correct way to work the bolt

Stores

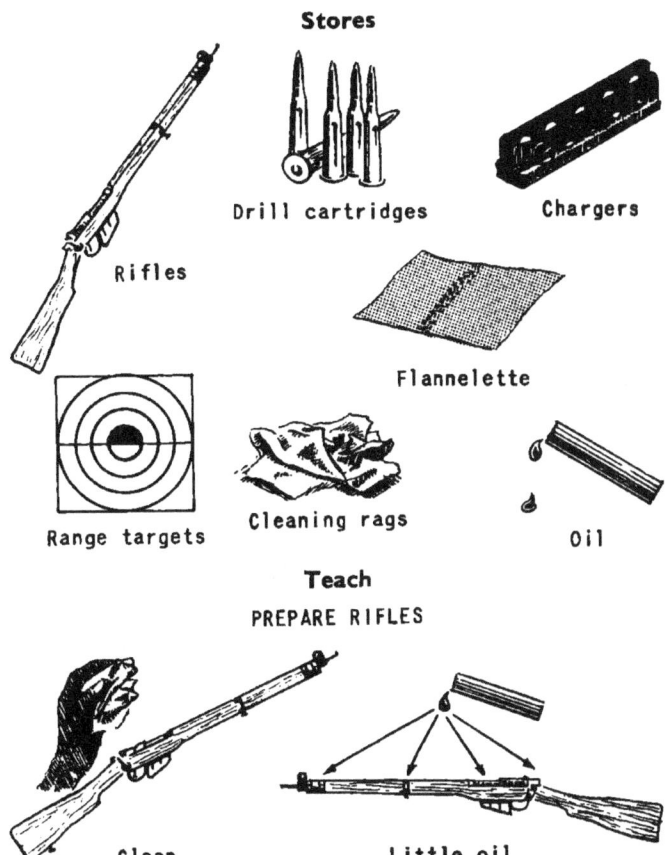

Teach
PREPARE RIFLES

Clean

Little oil

RELOADING

The lying position

Drill cartridges

Grasp bolt head with thumb and forefinger

Pull back as far as it will go and tilt to right

Close breech

Put hand on small of butt

Practise squad

Start off first by firing from the shoulder
and reloading at rest

Fire

Reload

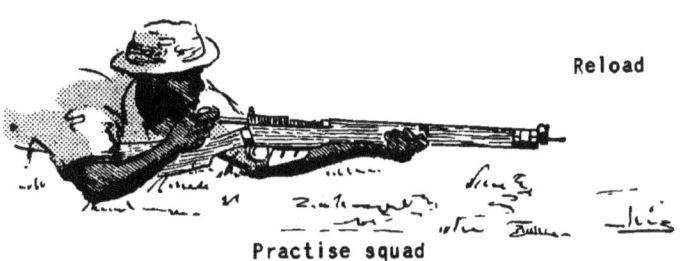

Practise squad

When squad can reload smoothly reload in the
shoulder

Fire

Reload

Practise squad

LESSON 13
FURTHER CLEANING

Extra cleaning **Lesson**

Stores

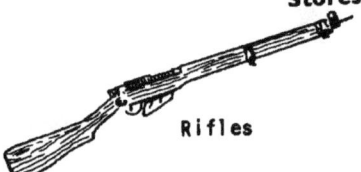
Rifles

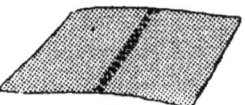
Flannelette

Cleaning rags

Pull-throughs

Wire gauzes

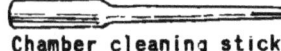
Chamber cleaning stick

Boiling out pots

Funnels

Linseed oil

Teach

The rifle will be very clean.   These must not have oil

Barrel - Dry

Gas Escapes - Dry

Chamber - Dry

Magazine - Dry

AFTER FIRING

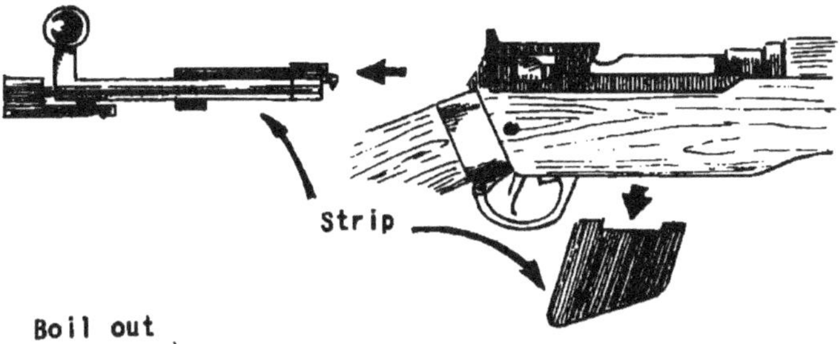

Strip

Boil out

Do not put water on the wood

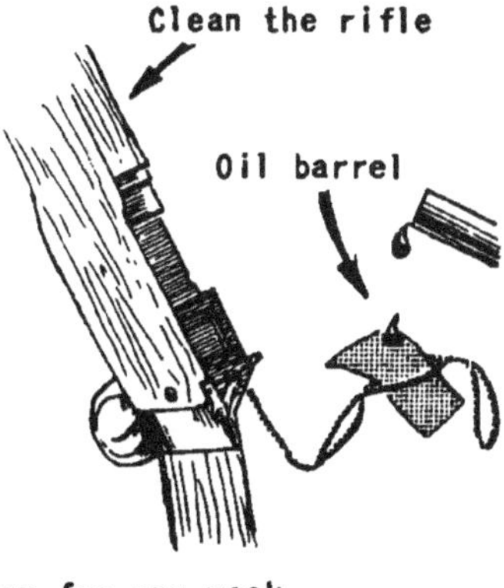

Clean the rifle

Oil barrel

Clean every day for one week

WIRE GAUZE

For cleaning worn barrels, gauze will be used only by order from an officer

To put on pull-through

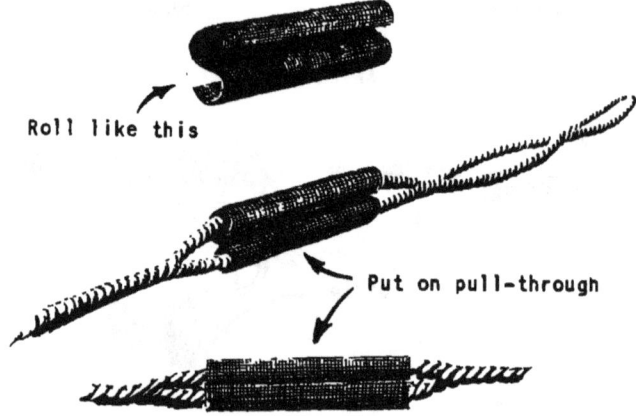

Roll like this

Put on pull-through

WOODWORK

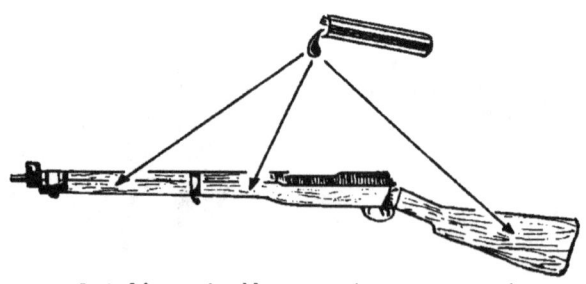

Put linseed oil on wood once a month

LESSON 14
SNAPSHOOTING

Lessons

Rapid aim
Taking a quick shot

Stores

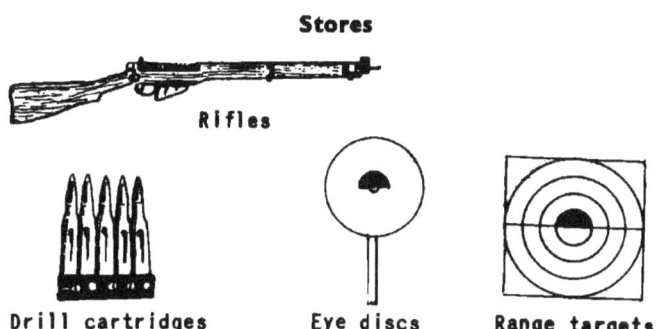

Rifles

Drill cartridges   Eye discs   Range targets

Teach
NO EYE DISC

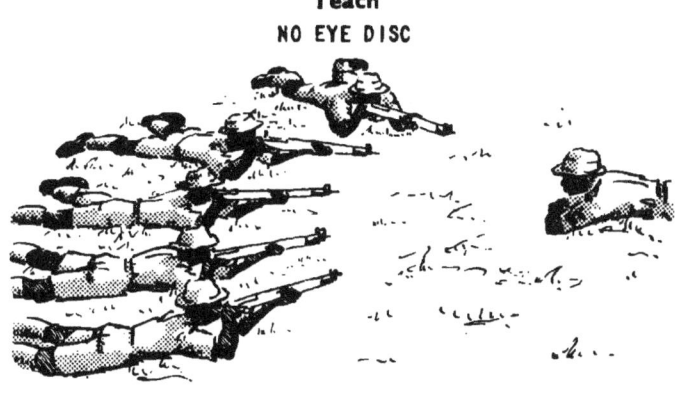

All in lying position.   Check for a steady aim

WITH EYE DISC

All in lying position. Practise with eye disc one by one

One man beside the instructor to practise rest of squad using small figure target.

SPEED

Elbows in correct place

Good grip on rifle

Quick aiming

Reload in shoulder

CHECK WITH EYE DISC

Practise squad

LESSON 15
RAPID FIRING

Lesson

To fire well aimed shots quickly

Stores

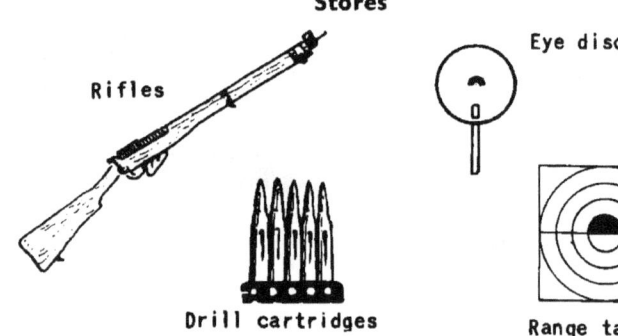

Rifles

Drill cartridges

Eye discs

Range targets

Teach

Commands "RAPID"

Rifle to shoulder

Aim

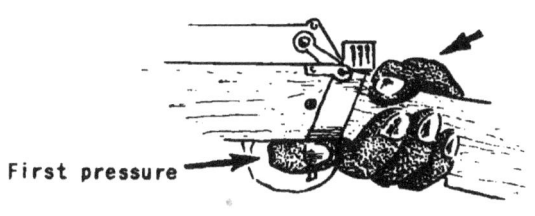
First pressure

"FIRE"

Pull trigger

Reload

Keep butt in shoulder when reloading

Work bolt smoothly

Fire and reload as fast as possible without losing aim

TEST SQUAD FOR:-

Speed

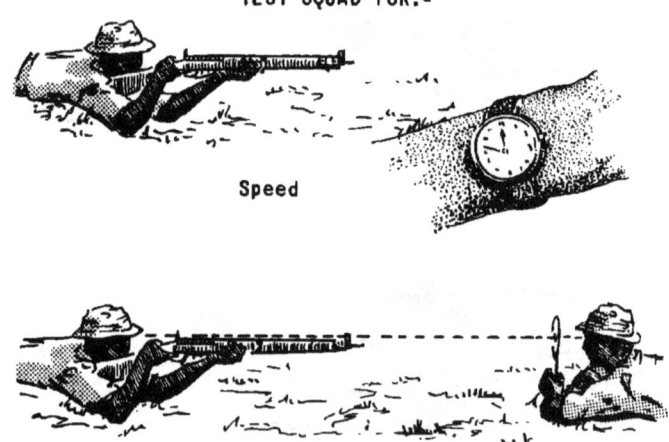

Aim

LESSON 16
THE TRAINING STICK

Lesson
To quicken up the soldier in bayonet training

Stores

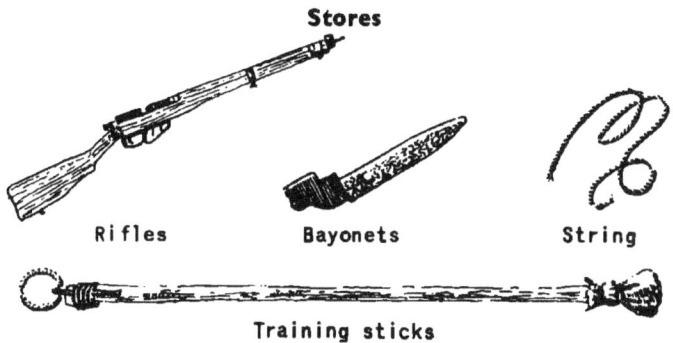

Rifles Bayonets String

Training sticks

Teach

Tie scabbard on

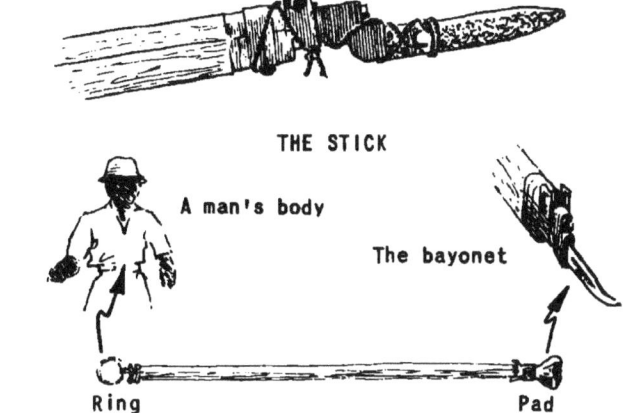

THE STICK

A man's body

The bayonet

Ring Pad

To point the pad means On Guard

The Ring means Point

Practise squad on guard and rest

Rest

On guard

POINTS ON RIGHT

One point

Two points

Take one pace back

Show squad using rifle and bayonet

One Point

Two Points

Practise squad

POINTS ON LEFT

One Point

Two points
Jump forward

Practise squad

LESSON 17
FIRING FROM OTHER POSITIONS

Lesson

The kneeling, sitting and standing positions

Stores

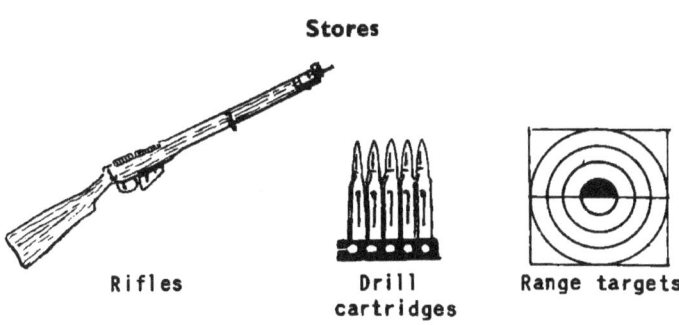

Rifles   Drill cartridges   Range targets

Teach

KNEELING

Pace forward with left foot
Rifle from right to left hand

Kneel on right knee

Hold rifle like this

Fire from this position

SITTING

Both elbows rested

Firing drill same as for lying position

STANDING

AIMING

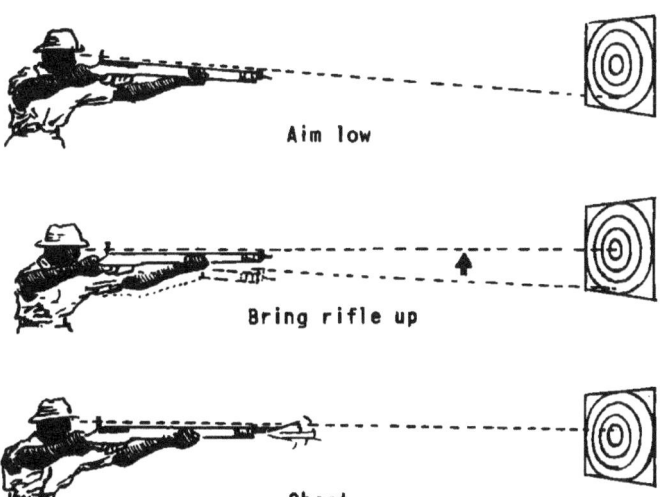

LESSON 18
SELF-DEFENCE

Lesson
To teach self-defence with the bayonet

Stores

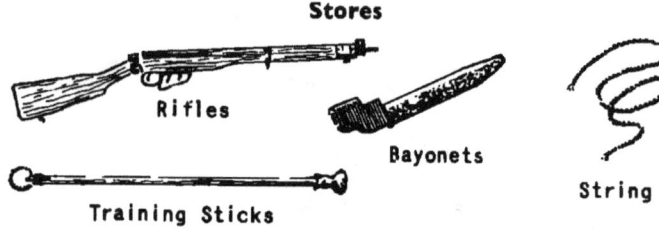

Rifles

Bayonets

Training Sticks

String

Teach
LEFT PARRY

Show squad

Butt stroke

Bayonet

Practise squad

RIGHT PARRY

Bayonet

Practise squad

W.O.
CODE NO.

| RESTRICTED | 8835-1 |

The information given in this document is not to be communicated, either directly or indirectly, to the Press or to any person not authorized to receive it.

26/GS Training Publications/2099

INFANTRY TRAINING

RIFLE AND BAYONET

1954

AMENDMENTS (No. 1)

MANUSCRIPT AMENDMENTS

1. Page 12   To left of 2nd diagram *insert* "Put in a second charger of 5 rounds."

2. Page 15   Line 1 *delete* "FILL" and *substitute* "CHARGE"

3. Page 28   *Above* "FIRING A SHOT" *insert* "Practise squad"

    Below "Put range on sights" *insert* "Push forward the safety catch"

4. Page 37   *Delete* "To correct errors in elevation" and *substitute* "When to alter sights"

    Delete "Aiming discs" and *substitute* "Eye discs"

5. Page 43   Last diagram ("Little oil"). *Delete* all arrows except that indicating the bolt.

6. Page 49   *Below* "NO EYE DISC" *insert* "NO DRILL CARTRIDGES"

7. Page 51   *Between* first and second diagrams *insert* "FIRE"

    After "Reload in shoulder" *insert* " — Aim again — Rest"

8. Page 53   Under second diagram *delete* "Pull" and *substitute* "Press"

9. Page 54   *Above* last line ("Aim") *insert* "NO DRILL CARTRIDGES"

CUT OUT AMENDMENTS

10. Page 2 *Delete* third diagram and *insert* new diagram below:—
    Amdt. 1/Nov./1955

Squeeze trigger

11. Page 13 *Delete* fourth diagram and *insert* new diagram below:—
    Amdt. 1/Nov./1955

Squeeze trigger

12. Page 24 *Delete* third diagram and *insert* new diagram below:—
    Amdt. 1/Nov./1955

EXERCISE I

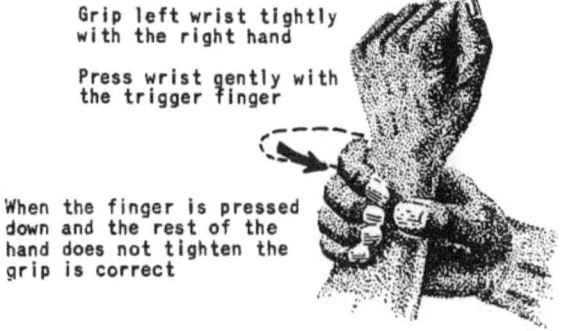

Grip left wrist tightly with the right hand

Press wrist gently with the trigger finger

When the finger is pressed down and the rest of the hand does not tighten the grip is correct

13. Page 29 *Delete* second diagram and *insert* new diagram below:-
    Amdt. 1/Nov./1955

14. Page 38 *Delete* first diagram and wording "At 300 yds each 100 yds change on backsight means this:-" and *insert* new diagram and wording below:-
    Amdt. 1/Nov./1955

At 300 yds each 100 yds change on backsight 4 ft target means this

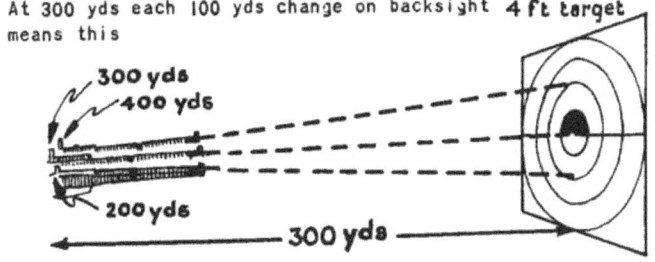

Practise squad

15. Page 62 *Delete* last two diagrams and *insert* two new diagrams below:—
Amdt. 1/Nov./1955

Show squad

Butt stroke

16. Page 63 *Delete* second diagram and *insert* new diagram below:—
Amdt. 1/Nov./1955

Bayonet

Practise squad

NEW PAGE
Amdt. 1/Nov./1955

17. *Delete* page 26 and *insert* new page 26 attached.

By Command of the Army Council

THE WAR OFFICE,
11th November, 1955.

DS 96470/1/8794 15,000 10/55 CL

LESSON 7
FIRING A SHOT

Lessons

To teach the drill for firing a shot
Prepare for miniature range

Stores

Rifles

Sandbags

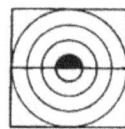
Targets

Drill cartridges

Teach

Ask squad for three rules of shooting

Sandbag

Show correct use of it. Like this

The sandbag is to steady the rifle. Support the lower part of the forearm only.
Practise squad

www.ingramcontent.com/pod-product-compliance
Lightning Source LLC
Chambersburg PA
CBHW060215050426
42446CB00013B/3077